Two By Two

Animals and Alphabets

Written by
LaJuana D Jackson

Illustrated by
Justin Perkins

Genesis 2:19,20

19 ... the LORD God formed every beast of the field, and every fowl of the air; and brought them unto Adam to see what he would call them: and whatsoever Adam called every living creature, that was the name thereof.
20 And Adam gave names to all cattle, and to the fowl of the air, and to every beast of the field;...

I dedicate this book to my sister Tane' Jackson.
God made so many wonderful things,
and you are one of the greatest things that He made.

Love you,

Sisters forever

To The Parents:

Thank you for choosing to spend quality time with your child using my book. I hope you and your child will enjoy reading Two by Two!

After you read the book, I pray that it sparks conversations with you and your child, so that you are able to edify them and tell them how God considers them one of the greatest things He has made. Build up your child spiritually and mentally. Tell them that God made some pretty cool and awesome animals, but nothing compares to them.

This book was also designed to be educational, which makes reading this book twice as much fun! This book introduces 3 educational topics; animals, the letters of the alphabet and sign language. Start by teaching your child about the animals that are in this book. By discussing animal behaviors, life lessons can be taught. For example, dogs are loyal and faithful. Ask your child how they can be loyal and faithful. Next, you can help your little one with the alphabet. Learning the alphabet teaches letter recognition, which enables beginning readers to be exposed to learning sounds, which will develop their language skills. Lastly, have fun learning another way to communicate.

Sign language will help your child start to develop their small motor skills.

My prayer is that Two by Two will entertain your child and help to inform them that God dearly loves and specially created them.

God made the animals two by two.

A

a

He made the **A**lligator,

and He made the **B**uffalo.

God made the animals two by two.

He made the **C**at,

D

d

and He made the Dog.

God made the animals two by two.

E

e

He made the **E**agle,

and He made the **F**ox.

God made the animals two by two.

G

g

He made the Giraffe,

H h

and He made the Horse.

God made the animals two by two.

He made the Iguana,

J j

and He made the Jaguar.

God made the animals two by two.

K k

He made the Kangaroo.

and He made the **L**lama.

God made the animals two by two.

M

He made the **M**onkey,

m

and He made the Newt.

God made the animals two by two.

O

He made the **O**strich,

O

and He made the Penguin.

God made the animals two by two.

Q q

He made the Quail,

R

and He made the Rhinoceros.

r

God made the animals two by two.

He made the Sheep,

T

and He made the Turtle.

God made the animals two by two.

U

He made the Umbrellabird,

and He made the **V**ulture.

God made the animals two by two.

W

He made the **W**hale,

and He made the Xiphosuran.
(Zif-uh-soo r-uh n)

God made the animals two by two.

He made the Yak,

and He made the Zebra.

God made all the animals two by two,

but the GREATEST thing God
made was me and you!

Made in the USA
Monee, IL
07 December 2019